Written and Illustrated
by
Shachar Edry

MW00902984

SHACHAR
and
KUTI

© Copyright 2018 Danielle Karten
ISBN: 13: 978-0-9994664-3-8
Text and Illustrations by Shachar Edry

All rights reserved. No part of this book may be reproduced, scanned, or distributed in any printed, or electronic form, including recording, photocopying, taping or by any information storage retrieval system now known or to be invented without the permission of the author except in the case of brief quotations embodied in critical articles and reviews in a magazine, newspaper or broadcast. Please do not participate in or encourage piracy of copyrighted materials in violation of the author's rights. Purchase only authorized editions.

Edited by Jim Bergman

Graphic Design by Chloe Annetts
www.chloeartdesign.com

Published by

MEDIACS

Also available as an eBook.

SPECIAL THANKS TO

Professor Alex Margolis
M.D., Director, Plastic Surgery Center, Hadassah Ein Kerem Hospital

Naomi Jabotafsky
M.D., the pediatrician who has cared for Shachar since she was born

The Yaldei ha'Or Foundation
A charity for children with nevus and their families (www.nevus.org.il)

Michal Tibika-Nadjer
emotional caregiver

Hava Migdal
Manager, Hartuv Elementary School

Ora Zevuluni
Shachar's teacher in first and second grade

Ramond Elias
Shachar's teacher in third and fourth grade

Limor Sinuani
Shachar's caretaker while she was illustrating this book

Hi. My name is Shachar.
I live in a community
overlooking the Elah Valley
in Israel. Today is my 10th
birthday. But I'm not the
only one celebrating. It's also
Kuti's 10th birthday today.
Kuti lives in my brain, just
behind my forehead.

5

I bet you're wondering...
Who is Kuti?

When I was born, my body was covered with giant beauty marks called nevi. When my three-year-old brother Or came to the hospital and met me for the first time, our parents Shlomi and Meirav told him everyone is born with something special. "A sign of uniqueness," they explained. Or was very happy. "I have a special sister," he bragged.

When I was six-months old, I started fainting a lot. One second, I would be doing something. A second later, I would wake up from a nap. After many hospital visits, the doctors discovered Kuti was living inside my head. Kuti, they said, was making me pass out. So the doctors gave me a special medication to stop me from fainting.

Kuti has a big family. She has a father, mother, grandfather, grandmother and ten brothers and sisters. They're all beauty marks, like Kuti. I have lots of other spots. On my legs, arms, stomach, back and other places on my body. But Kuti is the only troublemaker because she lives in my brain. Sometimes Kuti makes me fall down. Sometimes she causes pain in my head.

There's a small door inside
my head so Kuti can come
and go as she pleases. But
she never leaves my head
for long.

Kuti loves her family. She visits them often. Her favorite thing to do is play hide-and-seek with her brothers and sisters after breakfast.

As I grew older, the doctors removed those beauty marks they thought could become cancer. They also put new, healthy skin on my body. Some of the operations were painful. But my parents and my doctors helped me relax and sometimes even smile.

I used to lose my temper at Kuti.

Why are you here?

I want you to disappear!

I want you to stop bugging me!

I wish you'd never been born with me!

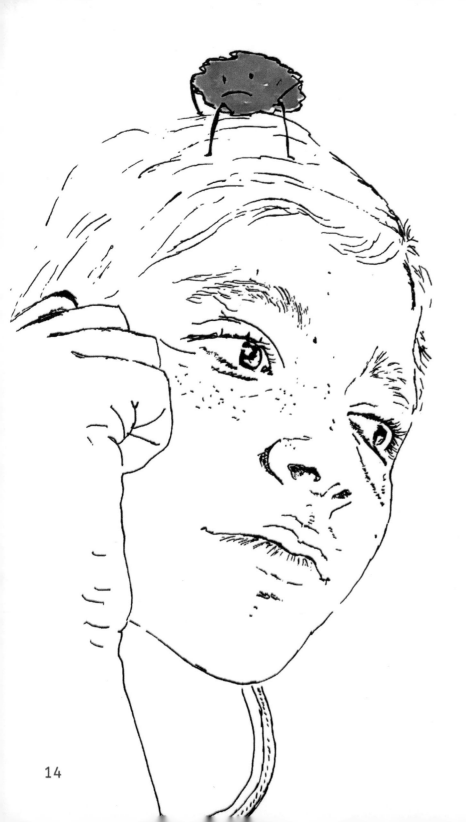

I once got so mad at her I screamed out loud. "Kuti, I'm going to break open my head, and toss you into the garbage. I want a normal head like my sister, Yalli." But then I felt really sad. Kuti is a part of me. I cannot just throw her away. I have to accept her. I have to learn how to live with her.

Now I hardly ever get mad at Kuti. She still gives me headaches. She still makes me fall down. She still worries my parents and doctors. But getting mad at her just makes everybody feel worse, especially me. And thanks to Kuti I've learned how to conquer my fear of painful skin surgeries and overcome my sadness and anger. I used to ask myself "Why am I the one who has to go through all of this?" I don't ask that anymore!

Sometimes I wonder why Kuti chose me. But I know that's not really important. All that matters is that she did choose me, and now we're together.

Kuti really likes to swim. Every time I dive into a pool, she gets really happy. I know Kuti loves me and doesn't want to live in any other kid's head.

17

Some kids pretend not to see my beauty marks when they meet me for the first time. Other kids are shocked or uncomfortable. If they ask me about my beauty marks, I tell them: "My spots are not normal, but I am. They are part of me, but not all of me. I love my friends, I go to school, I belong to a scout troop, I swim. I'm really just like you!"

I also love to draw which is one of the reasons I decided to make this book. I also wanted to tell everybody about Kuti, my most troubling spot.

When I went to the hospital, which was often, I met many other children with beauty marks like mine. The spots could be anywhere on the body. Some were huge. Some were tiny. Some were dark. Some were light. But they were all spots. That's what we kids with nevi share in common.

One day, I asked Doctor Margolis, who works at the hospital, to organize a party for all of us kids with birthmarks and our parents. Our first party was at my home a few weeks later. Everybody had a really good time. We still get together often.

For our 10th birthday, I asked Kuti to fulfill just one wish: please stay little and not grow. That way she will not bother my head too much, and we can keep on living together. That's our deal. She'll be with me, and I'll be with her. She'll love me, and I'll love her. She'll stand by me, and I'll stand by her.

Today, Kuti and I are celebrating our 10th birthday. My parents are giving us a birthday party. Kuti is not growing bigger! She's shrinking! Which makes everybody a lot happier.

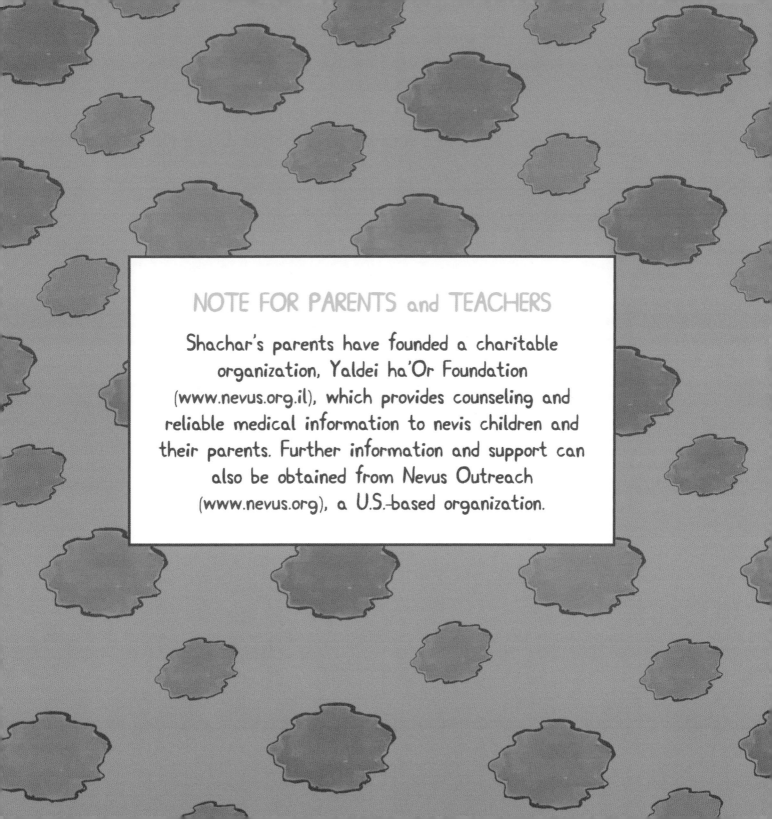

NOTE FOR PARENTS and TEACHERS

Shachar's parents have founded a charitable organization, Yaldei ha'Or Foundation (www.nevus.org.il), which provides counseling and reliable medical information to nevis children and their parents. Further information and support can also be obtained from Nevus Outreach (www.nevus.org), a U.S.-based organization.

Proof

Made in the USA
Columbia, SC
07 August 2018

23323611R00015